*A*lways remember...
listen to your heart,
trust what you hear,
and do what you believe is right.

Other Books by Donna Fargo
Published by
Blue Mountain Arts®

I Prayed for You Today:
A Collection of Uplifting Thoughts
to Let Someone Special Know
How Much You Care

To the Love of My Life:
A Collection of Love Poems

Trust in Yourself:
Thoughts About Listening to Your
Heart and Becoming the Person
You Want to Be

Ten
Golden Rules
for Living
in This Crazy,
Mixed-Up
World

Donna Fargo

Blue Mountain Press®

Boulder, Colorado

Library of Congress Control Number: 2006007497
ISBN-13: 978-1-59842-166-8
ISBN-10: 1-59842-166-2

Certain trademarks are used under license.
BLUE MOUNTAIN PRESS is registered in U.S. Patent and Trademark Office.

Printed in the United States of America.
First Printing: 2006

 This book is printed on recycled paper.

This book is printed on fine quality, laid embossed, 80 lb. paper. This paper has been specially produced to be acid free (neutral pH) and contains no groundwood or unbleached pulp. It conforms with the requirements of the American National Standards Institute, Inc., so as to ensure that this book will last and be enjoyed by future generations.

Library of Congress Cataloging-in-Publication Data

Fargo, Donna.
      Ten golden rules for living in this crazy, mixed-up world / Donna Fargo.
          p. cm.
      ISBN 1-59842-166-2 (trade pbk. : alk. paper)
      1. Conduct of life.   I. Title.

BJ1581.2.F29 2006
158—dc22

                              2006007497

Blue Mountain Arts, Inc.

P.O. Box 4549, Boulder, Colorado 80306

Ten Golden Rules for Living in This Crazy, Mixed-Up World

1. **KNOW WHO YOU ARE AND WHAT YOU'RE DOING HERE.** Recognize that you are special and unique. Your life is a gift to you. Appreciate this gift with all your heart, and be the best you can be.

2. **KNOW WHAT YOU WANT OUT OF LIFE AND WHAT YOU WANT TO CONTRIBUTE.** Believe in yourself and your dreams. Come up with a plan, be willing to change if something isn't working, but never stop reaching for your goals. Keep trying until you succeed.

3. **TAKE CARE OF YOURSELF.** Respect your body. It's the only one you have. Eat healthy foods, drink lots of water, and get plenty of exercise. Know that you are spirit, mind, and body. Educate them all.

4. **REALIZE THAT YOU ARE NOT ALONE.** God lives in your very own heart. Pray to Him often, listen to His guidance, and don't forget to thank Him for your blessings.

5. **NEVER UNDERESTIMATE THE POWER OF LOVE.** Choose to love others, for when you show love, you are not only helping yourself, but also making a positive difference in other people's lives.

6. **LIVE YOUR LIFE IN A SPIRIT OF COOPERATION WITH OTHERS.** Treat others as you would want to be treated, no matter how they've treated you. Don't judge others or try to change them. You'll have enough trouble changing yourself.

7. **TREASURE THE SPECIAL PEOPLE IN YOUR LIFE.** They teach us some of life's most important lessons. They teach us about love. They search with us for life's meaning. They help us to have faith.

8. **LIFE WILL HURT SOMETIMES, BUT YOU CAN HANDLE IT.** Face problems head-on, and make the best of everything. When you're down, get up and try again. Know that whatever you're going through will look different on another day.

9. **COUNT YOUR BLESSINGS.** Enjoy the simple things in life — the things you can't buy. When you're not happy with yourself, find something in your life that you appreciate. When there's no sunshine in your life, make your own.

10. **CHOOSE TO BE HAPPY.** Embrace life and enjoy it. At all times, find something to be thankful for. Celebrate each and every day. Steadfastly refuse to let anything steal your joy.

INTRODUCTION

My greatest goal in writing this book is to help you view your life as a beautiful gift. As you explore these ideas, I hope they will help you see that you really are a very special creation, you matter to the world, you have a purpose here, and you can make a positive difference. I encourage you to become friends with your inner voice so you can evaluate whether you're really being who you want to be and doing all that you're capable of doing.

In this crazy, mixed-up world, I think we need a code of ethics to help us get along better. Although I mention God in this book because I believe in God, I am not advocating a particular religion. I believe your religion is your business, but I do suggest getting to know the God in your heart. For me, doing so has been vital and life enhancing, and I have benefited from knowing the power of His love.

I also believe people need to develop a way of thinking that supports creative independence and the courage to become involved in making our world a better place. For most of us, determining and practicing what we believe is a process, so having the "right" belief system for yourself is only the first step. Action is required to get desired results. That's the hard part. As we find peace in our small worlds, we contribute to the good of the bigger world we live in by being angels in disguise to some, friends to others, and treasured loved ones to members of our families.

Being faced with a serious health problem directed me to put more emphasis on my health and caused me to reach some of the conclusions I share with you in this book. I also learned some of my greatest lessons by being a high school English teacher, and my varied experiences as an entertainer, recording artist, and songwriter have further influenced my thinking.

I believe that a happy, productive life starts with a healthy relationship with ourselves. An enlightened, educated spirit in proper sync with our minds and bodies moves us toward an emotional security in which almost anything is possible and nothing can steal our joy, no matter what's going on around us.

Although we live in a fast-changing society and sometimes impersonal and unfriendly world, I encourage you to stay grounded, keep your focus, and never lose sight of what's valuable. Be very diligent and cautious about how you adjust to the changes that occur. Amidst the noise and clutter, take time to camp out in your own heart on a regular basis. Realize that there's magic in your desires. Examine the principles that are creating your legacy, and always focus on doing exactly what you believe is right for you.

Through all the distractions in this crazy, mixed-up world, live as though your life is sacred and precious and meaningful and important in the whole scheme of things... because it is.

— Donna Fargo

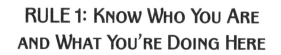

RULE 1: KNOW WHO YOU ARE AND WHAT YOU'RE DOING HERE

A fulfilled life starts with knowing who you are, and our uniqueness is our first gift. We are spiritually, mentally, and physically distinct. There is no one in the world like you. Imagine! Take time each day to be grateful for your life.

Be thankful for your talents. Use them or risk losing them; they cowrite with you the melodies in your heart. Be actively involved in the pursuit of your goals. They drive you and make life interesting and fun.

Be honest with yourself about your weaknesses and your strengths. Know what inspires you. Don't give stress any power over you; it's unhealthy and a waste of your time. Talk to yourself and follow your advice.

Never forget where you came from. Your family and childhood experiences have influenced you. Knowing your background will help you to understand yourself better, and making peace with any family issues will make it easier for you to do what you want to do with your life.

Focus on the Positive

Ignore all the ways you put yourself down for a moment and focus on your positive characteristics. Think about how you are living up to your expectations. Examine your attitudes, accomplishments, and the things that make you glad you're you and not somebody else. Are you thoughtful and sensitive to others' needs? Do you accept people and make them feel comfortable? If these are virtues and assets in your case, give yourself credit.

Process any negative impressions you have about yourself. Don't get bogged down in past defeats, but don't keep making the same mistakes either. If you're not happy with yourself, start changing.

Our thoughts can hold us back or set us free. When we concentrate too much on why we don't have a chance, we recycle negativity into our belief system and we keep getting what we've been getting. If you're having a hard time believing something you know you need to believe, say, "I want to believe that; I'm willing. Help me."

Don't get caught up in just taking what you can get and letting life live you. Your heart is your center; your intentions reside there, alongside your personal power to turn them into reality. Have a healthy pride in yourself.

I love it when I see a little tree or flower coming up through the gravel in the road. It helps my faith. The seed probably didn't see all those rocks when it blew in there, but it wasn't afraid. It didn't ask permission. It just grew. And have you ever wondered what a little bird says before it takes flight? Probably nothing. It just flies. Are you for you or against you?

Be Thankful for the Family
You Were Born Into

Sometimes we take our families for granted, and love should start at home. Whether you came about by desire or accident and no matter how functional or dysfunctional your childhood was, it is important to your psychological health to accept and love your family unconditionally.

When you make a conscious choice to love rather than withhold acceptance, you are nourishing your own health, as well as the other person's. When people don't act the way you think they should, love them anyway. You don't need to atone for their mistakes. You are responsible for yourself, and they are responsible for themselves. Love without requiring anything in return. If family members are adding stress to your life, it's because you are allowing them to, so you must let it go. You can't change them anyway, even if they're wrong, and everyone has a right to be wrong.

On a personal note, I had a number-one single called "You Were Always There." I wrote the song for my mother after she died — too young, in her fifties — and I realized that there was so much about her life that I didn't know. I encourage you to get to know your family because you never know when they won't be around. They can help you fit together the pieces of the puzzle of your life and give you the opportunity to bring joy to their lives.

Both the desirable traits and some of the undesirable traits of your family have had an effect on you. You wouldn't be who you are without them, and they wouldn't be who they are without you. The family is a small world in which each person has a unique role and the right to be who he or she is. How you manage your family relationships will help you define who you are and contribute to the final grade you give yourself in life.

Learn from Others, but Be Yourself

You've been influenced by your family, school, religious upbringing, and society. At some point, you need to analyze how all these influences have caused you to evolve into the person you are. Don't think someone else's thoughts or say someone else's words or be constantly caught up in trying to please others. It's a good idea to listen to others and evaluate what they say and do because we learn from one another, but always be true to yourself and know your own beliefs and feelings. Don't ever just go along with the crowd to be accepted. You know in your heart what's right and wrong for you. Remember that, whether you're "talked into" a situation or do something of your own volition, you will be held accountable just the same.

Rather than let others be the measure of your success, compare your achievements with your own potential, not someone else's. Observe what comes easily for you, what you enjoy. Ask yourself what you like to do most of all and then do those things as well as you can. See your potential as unlimited, and be in a continuous stage of growth. If you fail at something, don't stop trying. Find new ways and different approaches to stay interested and contribute to your own development.

Appreciate the teaching and example of others, but don't just do what others have done. Be thankful for the special qualities that you have and for the grace by which you've received them. Accept them with humility and share them freely.

Be the Best "You" That You Can Be

Once you've identified what makes you unique, commit yourself to being the best that you can be. The more you practice your talent and cultivate your specialty, the happier you will be and the more creative you'll become in applying yourself. Give of yourself and reach out to others.

Do the best that you can and accept that as enough. Be yourself; you're no better or worse than anyone else. You know what you can do, so set your own limits. Think your own thoughts. Dream your own dreams. Make your own plans. Do your own thing. Make your actions line up with what you really believe. You are depending on you. Have confidence in yourself, and don't let yourself down.

Everything may not always seem to work out for the best for you, but you can make the best of everything. What you do in response to the detours and surprises in life — the things you didn't plan — help to define who you are. Don't be afraid. Know that you will deal with the roadblocks that life puts in your way and you will be wiser as a result of these challenges.

Whether your life is moving along according to your plans or fate is taking you somewhere else, how you play the cards you're dealt is another golden opportunity for you to be the best "you" that you can be.

If you find yourself "burning out" or needing a change, find a new "slant" on exercising your talent before you lose interest. Talent needs the freedom to grow, and life is more interesting when you're engaged and productive and progressive.

Take Charge of Your Life

Among the choices that have been made for us are our race, color, nationality, gender, and the family we were born into. Because we had no say in these, we are not inferior or superior to anyone else. We are just ourselves. When there is no choice, prejudice toward anyone should not be an option.

Accept yourself as you are, and be comfortable in your own skin. Discover everything you've been entrusted with, and take responsibility for your life.

You are the perfect dreamer of your dreams. They chose your heart to live in and your life to bless, and they want to come true for you. You are the one who is writing your story, and there are beautiful surprises and marvelous wonders waiting for you just over the horizon.

Don't allow yourself to get lost in all the distractions in the world. Turn off the noise and visit with your own silence. Allow yourself to tap into that source of power that lives inside your heart and lets you sail to the depths and heights of who you are and become all that you can imagine. Appreciate the awesome beauty of nature and humanity; it will inspire you to give more of yourself.

On the sunrise of your future, life is on your side. It wants the best for you; live each day with pleasure and dignity. Use your energy wisely. Your story is a masterpiece unfolding, and the hero of your story is you.

RULE 2: KNOW WHAT YOU WANT OUT OF LIFE AND WHAT YOU WANT TO CONTRIBUTE

We each move to life's ever-changing rhythms with a melody of our own, and we are constantly adjusting to our heart's own compass. Whether you have aspirations of becoming a rock star or finding a cure for cancer, the desire in your heart will direct you toward satisfaction and fulfillment, if you listen.

Your purpose and your dreams belong to you; they help define you. Handle them with care; have confidence in your thoughts and actions. Be flexible and open. Dreams don't always come with maps to get us to where we want to go, and we may not always recognize a turn we need to take. Get all the experience you can related to the field you're interested in. It's important that you love what you do and that you're good at it.

By knowing what you want to give and receive from life, you form a philosophy that you can live your life by. Make sure you're living by the principles you believe in and not just thinking or talking about them.

Don't Waste Your Time

We know when we were born, but since we don't know when we'll die, the time we have to work with is a mystery. This unknown factor is what should cause all of us to hold every moment close and enjoy life every day, no matter where we are in our journey. Too often people are just cruising along, taking life for granted, and acting as though they're going to live forever.

Some people don't enjoy the present because they are constantly thinking about the past or the future. Others waste their time dwelling on what they hate so much that they've lost track of what they love. Instead of using their energy to make their dreams come true, some stay stuck in the dream. They're safe there. Nothing's required of them. Some people think "I'd be so happy if…" this or that would happen. Don't ever put off being happy, even if your dream never comes true. Dreams are important, but we are more than our dreams. Life is the prize. Things could always be worse. Be happy no matter what, and always be thankful for the blessings you do have.

The wonderful thing about life is we have the power to change at least some things that we're unhappy with. Become friends with that power. Increase your level of awareness and get your actions in line with your goals. I'm not saying change is easy, but it's possible. And you learn so much about yourself when you see a need and you try to make a change. Use your time wisely to accomplish what you want to do with your life. Discover your purpose and pursue your dreams. You're the only one who can!

Start Now

Don't wait for lightning to strike, magic to happen, or someone to do something for you. Devise a plan based on what your heart, feelings, and mind are telling you, and start somewhere. While you may require the help of others, you will ultimately be responsible for whether you win or lose and how you will prevail. You can't expect someone else to give up his or her life for you to achieve your goals.

Be sure you have the knowledge and education you need. Don't just learn enough to get by. Become an expert about what you're interested in. You may have to try different approaches and angles. Remember, it's better to be prepared and have to wait for the right opportunity than to have the opportunity and not be prepared.

If it's a new job you desire, talk to people who are successful in the field you're interested in and listen to what they have to say. If at all possible, get some experience so you won't be surprised. Be sure the main assets required for the position are those that you have. For example, if you want to be a nurse or doctor, do you have the ability to make life-and-death decisions? Don't ever let money be the only reason for choosing an occupation.

Don't only be a thinker and a talker and a dreamer. Be a doer. Make the preparations you need to. Once you've done all you can, release your wishes and efforts to the impartial universe and allow the power of belief to do its work for you. Always remember that… you are the architect of your future and you are the one who should design the blueprint for your life.

Live Your Purpose
and Go for Your Dreams!

Once you know your purpose or begin to pursue your dreams, listen to them for direction. They're yours and yours alone. Own them. Don't settle for something less than you're capable of, but don't set your goals higher than you're equipped to reach either. Believe in yourself.

It may be that you'll find out something about yourself and your destiny by taking detours at times. A lot of life is left to chance. Get in touch with your intuition, and trust in yourself.

If you don't succeed at first, try again. Be patient. You will learn something from each effort. You can't be too prepared, so plan ahead.

Don't give up if you fail. If the hunger in your heart remains, it can be satisfied. Keep your desire burning. Feed it with enthusiasm, experience, effort, and confidence; have faith in your thoughts, words, and actions.

Visualize the job done and your dream come true. Imagine what a photograph taken at the time of your success would look like. See it enclosed in the perfect frame. Write your speech of gratitude. Fantasize. Only the universe and you will be listening. And don't forget to say "thank you."

If you want something enough to make changes in your life to get it, like changing a bad habit or devoting time and effort to learning something new, this show of sacrifice may be just when your purpose will be realized or your dream will trust you enough to come true. It is the dream that judges whether or not your efforts are enough, and it is the purpose that determines if you're headed in the right direction. If you give your best, you are to be congratulated. You've done all you can.

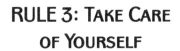

RULE 3: TAKE CARE OF YOURSELF

The healthier you are physically, mentally, and spiritually, the more you'll enjoy life and contribute to the lives of others. The happier you are, the more inspired you'll be to reach your optimum level of achievement.

Taking care of yourself means feeding your body the right foods, being careful what you feed your mind, and learning to process your feelings, based on the truths of your own experiences.

When I was diagnosed with multiple sclerosis in 1978, I instinctively knew that my body must be out of sync to be in a state of "dis-ease." I began educating myself about the spirit, mind, and body, and, in particular, diet. If you are struggling with an illness, I urge you to research your options. If you are healthy but have a tendency toward certain health problems, remember that preventing a problem will always be easier than healing a disease after it has had time to manifest.

Protect and value your life. Become proactive. Don't play games with yourself. Make wise choices. Take care of yourself.

Respect Yourself

Respect your body enough to stop doing things that hurt your health. Come to terms with harmful cravings and addictions. For example, if you smoke, consider whether or not the pleasure you get out of it is worth the risk of dying from lung cancer. Try to understand what your harmful habits symbolize for you, and come up with a plan to tackle them. Get to know yourself.

Respect your mind and watch what you feed it. Thoughts are like seeds; they will grow when nourished and die when left unattended. Your thoughts and actions have a cumulative effect on you. Take responsibility for them, and choose responses that promote good health and extend life.

Respect your feelings. They are your composite response system to everything that has influenced you. They filter all the things you've come in contact with. Sometimes feelings are reliable and sometimes they are not, but right or wrong, they are *your* feelings, so respect them, question them, and understand them. You will learn a lot about yourself by noticing your feelings.

Respect your spirit. It is the real you. It sees without seeing, knows without evidence, and loves without having to be loved. It is not limited by the five senses. It does not play games with you, and it knows what's best for you. It will help you keep a careful guard over your attitude and behavior and rise above them. Your mind can misunderstand and your feelings can be hurt, but your spirit will direct your mind and emotions for your own good, if you listen.

Look at your life with thankfulness. Do everything you can to achieve health for your body, satisfaction in your soul, commitment to what's important, and joy in each new day.

Maintain a Healthy Body

The state of your health often determines how long and how satisfying your life will be. Since a person can live about five weeks on average without food, several days without water, and only minutes without air, these are the absolute essentials we must have to live. So we influence our physical health and life span for better or worse by the quality of what we take into our bodies.

The body is continually renewing itself. Depending on the state of our health, the genes we inherit, and the energy we get from the foods we eat: about every three months we each get a new bloodstream; in eleven months we get new cells thoughout our bodies; our bones rebuild themselves about every two years. So within three years' time, the total body has gone through a process of renewal. We recycle ourselves! Can you see that if we started making healthier choices what a difference we could perhaps make in our health? Maybe the reason some people stay sickly is that they keep recycling the results of their habits and diets that they don't change.

If for no other reason than to maintain a comfortable weight, we need to have a healthy relationship with food. The mantra "eat to live; don't live to eat" is a good one. Ideally, we should eat only when we're hungry, instead of eating mindlessly.

We're spoiled. Certain foods have been used as rewards for so long... "If you're good, you can have some ice cream... I've had a bad day, so I deserve this piece of pie." We need to think about food differently. We need to eat to maintain a healthy body, not just to treat ourselves.

Resolve to start making healthy lifestyle choices. To break bad habits, figure out a success mechanism that will work for you. Start by altering your mindset. You know yourself better than anyone, and it's important that you come up with your own plan based on what you will actually do. If you have tried to change something before and failed, shift your method. Stop one bad habit at a time and replace it with a good one. When these two changes are made, choose another two. Every small success you have will symbolize progress to you.

Determine what makes you do what you do, and deal with the problem. If you're overeating, you could be holding on to resentment toward someone for not showing you love, and you may be trying to fill a void that food cannot fill. You could be sabotaging yourself because of low self-worth. Maybe you don't think you deserve to be slim and healthy, or maybe you just need to exercise more discipline. Don't judge yourself too harshly. You didn't choose to be this way intentionally.

It's a good habit to commit to an exercise program for at least twenty minutes a day, three times a week. Fit the exercise to you and your body. For most people, walking is a healthy activity for the body and the soul. Also, because the body is over 60 percent water, remember to drink six to eight glasses of water a day.

We hear the words, "Do everything in moderation," and that sounds good, but you're the only one who can decide if you're "moderating" enough and how many risks you want to take concerning diet. The body is an amazingly forgiving machine, but we do need to honor it if we expect it to keep performing for us satisfactorily.

RULE 4: REALIZE THAT YOU ARE NOT ALONE

Know that you are a spiritual being, not just a body, mind, and soul. Realize that you are not alone, no matter how you feel sometimes. God lives in your heart. He may be perceived differently by everyone. That is okay. Get to know the God in *your* heart. Talk to Him; pray to Him. He is your connection to your higher self.

When I was a little girl, I was too afraid of God, so I had to "un-learn" the impression that I wasn't good enough for God to love me. I eventually realized that it was my own fear-based thinking that had me bound. Now I like to think of God as the one who cares about me and loves me with an everlasting love and who lets me know that I don't have to be perfect. It just feels right to me to associate everything about God with love, so love has become a truth to my soul. Once you acknowledge God in your heart, you will never feel alone and you will know that love is your greatest ally.

Educate Yourself Spiritually

Because your spirit is the real you, it's so important to educate yourself spiritually. You're just better off with your body, mind, and spirit working at their optimum. Imagine our society if we didn't go to school for at least twelve years to educate ourselves intellectually and to improve ourselves socially, mentally, and physically. Often people wait until there is a crisis in their lives to develop themselves spiritually. It really doesn't make any sense to neglect the development of our spirits.

The world's religious traditions are full of great guidebooks for us all to live by. Find one that speaks to your heart and study it — it's the best way I know to educate yourself spiritually. These books all share certain things in common. They teach us how to walk in love and how to live our lives. They tell us to be kind, to love our enemies, not to judge them, to do good to those who hate us, and to pray for those who use us. These are all good lessons to help us get along better and to achieve our dreams.

Some might ask "Why should I read books like these?" A better question might be "Why not?" We require reading of great novels in school. I like the word "desire" rather than "require," and they should be read with an open mind and heart to get the most benefit. You'll wind up with some thoughts and ideas that can help guide your life. These books were written for the very purpose to educate you spiritually and help you live your life in your best interest. Going to a house of worship and listening to faith-building recordings are very helpful, too, for your spiritual growth.

Faith Is So Important

Faith is a mystery that, if nurtured, can help you to become your best self and get your desires and needs met. Faith is like the still, small voice of God confirming that you're right about what you think you believe; it's an awareness of the existence of something that is essential to who you are. Faith is believing with all your heart that whatever you're hoping for will be realized. It's the voice of God that lives in your heart to encourage you.

We usually base our faith on lessons we've been taught, scriptures we've read, and thoughts we've held in our hearts until they have become truths to us. We can increase our faith by believing that we are more than our humanistic selves, by renewing our minds with spiritual truths, and by putting our spirits in charge. When we really believe, our faith will translate our hopes into reality.

So... don't get out of bed, face a new day, or go anywhere without faith. Don't hope or dream without it. Don't make a change or try to come up with a plan without it. Tell your doubts that you choose confidence instead. Tell your fears that you choose to have the courage to believe. Once you've made up your mind and your heart is in agreement, there's no stopping you. Hold on to your dream, your conviction, your hope, your goal. Don't fret. Don't panic. Just trust and believe.

Ask for your desires. Believe that God wants the best for you and that if you do what He tells you, you'll get what you want. Your faith will be the sunshine that the wishes in your heart absolutely must have to grow.

Walk in Love and Trust in Prayer

No matter what religion you associate yourself with, most of us know the importance of respecting life, love, and mankind. The keynotes in spiritual development always are to walk in love and pray in faith. You are walking in love when you pray for those you care about. Pray for their safety and well-being. Pray for them when they're having health issues. Pray that no accident or harm will come to them and that their problems will be solved in the most beneficial and painless way. Ask ahead of time for divine protection when someone is going to the hospital or taking a trip. Be very specific about your requests. Pray for their safe journey and return, free even of inconvenience. Pray also for yourself when you have problems to solve and need divine guidance. Then rest in the fact that you will receive because you have asked.

Pray in faith when you're trying to resolve a conflict with someone. You may not feel like praying about the situation or for the person involved, but you will feel better if you do pray. If you don't believe it, just experiment. The next time you're angry with someone or your feelings have been hurt, pray for the person, and observe the change of heart that comes over you.

Prayer humbles us and softens our sharp edges. It puts the spirit in charge and helps us to walk in love. It not only eases tension to make us feel better, but it also generates results for ourselves and for others.

And, finally, we need to pray that our leaders will make right decisions to save our planet and to achieve peace and discourage war. Our prayers could make a difference in our world.

Always Tell Yourself
the Truth

Not telling yourself the truth is the fastest way to inhibit your growth and prevent the gradual unfolding of your higher self. The more truthful you are with yourself, the more you open up your life to truth's healing light.

After what seemed to be millions of failed attempts to quit smoking and almost a total loss of self-respect, I began listening to what I was saying to myself: "You are such a weakling. You're never going to do this. You might as well give up." I soon realized that I wouldn't even talk to an enemy like that. No wonder I couldn't get the job done. I hadn't been telling myself the truth.

Then I began to say things to myself like: "Of course you can do this. Others have done it. You've accomplished other things. If you made a habit, you can break it." I was on my way, and ultimately I won the battle. It wasn't easy, but my road to victory over that addiction started with telling myself the truth.

If you're struggling with some issue, observe the conversations you're having with yourself. What are you saying over and over? If you call yourself a dummy or a failure long enough, you'll believe it and you'll slow your progress; conversely, if you act and speak truthfully, you will eventually succeed. Watch your language. Tell yourself the truth and you will change your belief. Then you will change your feelings about yourself, and finally you will change your behavior. It is our interpretation of events that recycles our feelings and creates the picture that will lead us to success or failure.

Seek Balance in
All Aspects of Your Life

As we strive to reach a higher ground, we also need to find a wholesome balance. Although putting the spirit in authority usually means the mind plays a more subservient role, we cannot deny its importance when we decide we want to change something about ourselves. For example, with clear insight and motivation, our weaknesses can turn into strengths, but with just a slight wrong turn of the wheel of common sense, our strengths may also become weaknesses.

Confidence is usually necessary to help you meet your goals, but if not checked and fine-tuned, too much of it can lead to arrogance. To avoid becoming egotistical and selfish, we need to blend confidence with humility and balance our thoughts and actions with a sincere concern for the well-being of others. On the other hand, to keep proper boundaries in your relationships, don't always put yourself last.

Most changes should start on the inside. Always trust your heart to guide you toward finding emotional equilibrium. Too little of anything may make us weak, but too much may make us extreme. If you are a workaholic and don't have any time for relaxation, your life is not in a state of harmony and you could be harming your health. Someone who is too loyal and determined can turn his passion into fanaticism, but someone with no loyalty will have a hard time winning the trust and friendship of others. It is the degree to which we exercise our freedom to be ourselves that may sometimes need adjustment to help us bring all aspects of our lives into proper sync.

RULE 5: NEVER UNDERESTIMATE THE POWER OF LOVE

Love is not just a word some poet made up. If you've ever loved anyone or been loved, you know how big love is. It's inside you, outside you, and everywhere. It's the one thing in life that has no limit. It is a never-ending source of power and the greatest gift we have all been given.

Love can open your heart to mysteries and wonders, put you in touch with the impossible, raise you out of mediocrity, and lift you to the heavens.

Think of it! Love costs nothing yet yields the greatest profit. Imagine a spring that cannot go dry, no matter how many wells it supplies.

That's the way love is. Once you allow yourself to love with all your heart, to walk without judgment, to accept without excluding, you have found the secret to happiness.

Love is a miracle we carry in our hearts. It can help us make a difference, influence our destiny, and transform our lives. How incredible it is to be able to love and be loved!

Love Can Change Your World

If only we could love enough, our hearts could direct us to do anything. We could change the world and heal the brokenhearted. No one would have to live afraid, go hungry, or suffer from lack or oppression. The desire for peace would erase the curse of war.

Love can help solve any problem and find an answer to any question. It creates its own language and lives inside every heart. When we are hurt, love is the best medicine for healing. It can get you over any walls and help you overcome any challenge.

Like food that is necessary to sustain the physical body, love feeds the spiritual self. It is like the blood of our spiritual father passed on to our hearts and souls to make us all the family of man. How could anyone hate when he's in touch with this love? How could it make us anything but peaceful and humble?

Love gives meaning and value to everything we are and expands the potential for the person we want to become. It can melt our most painful heartaches, overcome the most injurious wrongs, and create something wonderful out of nothing. It is the key that unlocks the secrets of the soul and the one thing in life we cannot afford to live without.

What a paradox it is that the more love we give, the more the supply is enlarged, the greater the return, and the richer our lives become. How blessed we are!

What Does It Mean to "Love Others as You Love Yourself"?

To love others as you love yourself means to put yourself in a position to feel someone else's pain and to treat that person as you'd hope to be treated if the same thing were happening to you.

But how should you love yourself? You should do this by having a deep respect for your life and then by treating others with the same respect. You should not feel superior, but rather have compassion for those who have done something "bad," remembering that our humanity makes us subject to the same misfortune. Our blessings should humble us, not make us feel superior to someone else.

Some of us take better care of our cars and favorite possessions than we do ourselves. If you love yourself, you'll take care of yourself. You'll say helpful things to yourself just as you would say to a friend. You will give yourself a pat on the back when you deserve it. You will find words to inspire yourself when you're depressed and need your own support.

Loving others means accepting them, encouraging them, and not judging them. Stop punishing yourself or someone else for something you wish had happened differently but can't be undone now. How many times should anyone pay for the same mistake? If you would wish for forgiveness, wouldn't you want to forgive? Love others and yourself.

You Were Born to Love and to Be Happy

If you have love in your heart but never show it, it's like having a present for someone and never giving it to that person. Don't withhold your love.

To find out how to show love, search your heart and acknowledge what matters to you. Reflect on how it feels when people are pleasant to you, considerate of you, and respectful toward you. What did they do or say to show their love? Was it an apology when you really needed it or an expression of appreciation when you helped someone? Did someone give you an opportunity that changed your life for the better? Think about the people in your favorite memories. What did they do to make you feel special? Let these examples teach you how to care for others.

If you want to be appreciated, you must show appreciation. If you want to be loved, you must show love. If you're unhappy with your life or your circumstances or upset with people much of the time, go inside your heart and do some soul searching. Ask for help in understanding yourself. Uncover the love inside your heart; let it feed you. You were born to love and to be happy. Pray a silent prayer to understand your situation and allow love to help you enjoy life more.

Your first call in life is to be an ambassador of goodwill. Let love live big inside you. Remember… what goes around comes around. Commit yourself to peace, love, and tolerance. If you do all these things, you will become all you're capable of.

Keys to Staying Happy
with the One You Love

First and foremost, love each other. Realize how lucky you are to be in love with someone who loves you. Accept each other completely. Don't take love for granted, ever. It's such a blessing.

Show your love in positive ways. Be a good listener. Watch your language. Don't take things personally. Say "I love you" often, and communicate lovingly and thoughtfully to each other.

Be sweethearts forever. Talk the way sweethearts talk. Do things to keep your love and romance new and alive and to make the other one feel loved. Stay fascinated with each other.

Take care of each other. Go to the doctor together. Put each other first, but don't neglect your own needs either. Share the chores. Work together. Support her dreams and respect his wishes.

Make the success of your relationship your greatest priority. Don't let your problems and concerns get out of hand and make you go in opposite directions. Be joyful that you've each made a commitment to the other and thankful you're in this life together.

Always be best friends. Talk about things together the way you would talk with a friend. Never betray each other's secrets; treat them as almost sacred. Give yourselves the freedom to express your opinions.

Be faithful to your partner. Settle the fact that you've made your choice and you're no longer looking for anyone else. Don't flirt. Think of the consequences. Don't ever give up on your love.

Keep your identity, but walk in agreement. Important decisions that affect you both should have the approval of both. Talk about how to manage your finances and work together. You double your strength when you're in agreement.

Treat the most important person in your life as you wish to be treated. If you've argued, never go to sleep without asking the other's forgiveness. Work through arguments in a spirit of love. Remember… you're sweethearts, best friends, and life partners. Act like it.

Have fun and enjoy life. It is important to have goals and work toward reaching them, but it's also very important to take time to relax and appreciate each other. Love each other and celebrate every day.

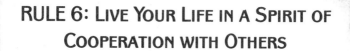

RULE 6: LIVE YOUR LIFE IN A SPIRIT OF COOPERATION WITH OTHERS

Practice the Golden Rule: "Do unto others as you'd have them do unto you." In all situations, ask yourself how you would want to be treated and treat others that way — your friends, family, enemies, children, strangers, coworkers — everyone!

Living in harmony with others could mean withholding judgment of someone. It could mean listening when someone needs to talk or saying something helpful or complimentary to someone who needs to hear it. It could mean agreeing with someone to show your approval or going out of your way to defend someone who needs defending.

Every person has the right to his or her own beliefs, and we each have our own needs and problems. It's not our business to try to change someone else, nor should we expect others to live up to our criteria.

When you allow people their differences, ultimately you will bring more joy and peace into your relationships. By adopting an attitude of acceptance and understanding, you are showing respect for the rights of the world family and living in a spirit of cooperation with others.

Put Yourself
in Other People's Shoes

Be sensitive to other people's needs and feelings; don't allow yourself to be prejudiced. Be present for someone who's going through a crisis. Share helpful ideas and options to show that there is a way out. Be supportive and compassionate.

Remember to say "I'm sorry" when you have said something hurtful to someone, especially someone you love. Also find the reason for your actions and begin to correct the problem as well as the symptom. One thing you can do to help you react to conflicts with the minimum amount of stress and the maximum amount of maturity is to train yourself to think before you respond. Don't just talk to be talking; you may say something you'll later regret. It's okay to say, "Let me think about that; I need some time on this issue."

Be considerate of other people's time. Keep your appointments. Call people when you're going to be late. They may have changed their schedule for you. Most people understand tardiness when they're informed of it. Communication is a good thing.

Give others the benefit of the doubt. Assume that people have good intentions and that they are not going to take advantage of you. Put yourself in other people's shoes sometimes, instead of expecting them to walk in yours.

How to Be More Beautiful
in a Not-So-Pretty World

For pretty eyes... see through the pain and conflict to find the goodness in all people. Look them straight in the eyes and be pleasant to them. They can see in your eyes that you care.

For a beautiful mouth... smile. A sincere smile means acceptance, and it's good for the giver and the receiver. Smile even at people you don't know; you could help to make someone's day. The feelings that your smile inspires in others will be stored in their memories and warm their hearts whenever it's recalled.

For better mental and spiritual fitness... ignore the grudges and the judgments of others. Share their burdens; find a common ground. Give what you can when you can. Lift them up; it helps them and you, too.

For a pretty nose... don't turn it upward. Humility will keep you on the right path. For soft skin... keep a soft heart. Be compassionate, loving, understanding, and tolerant. Your face will genuinely glow. For attractive ears... just listen well, and let what you hear also come through the heart.

For a memorable voice... speak encouraging words that offer hope and optimism. Don't hold back a compliment when it's deserved. It could make someone's day. Always speak kindly. Treat others the way you wish they'd treat you, and you will be beautiful to everyone you meet.

Be Generous with Your Kind Words

Words are so powerful. They can inspire a person to greatness, break someone's heart, or make someone angry. When we're down, words can pick us up; when we're up, they can let us down.

Words have such influence that they can make someone feel loved, appreciated, and accepted, or hated, disregarded, and ridiculed. They can help or hurt, make a person feel big or small. They can make the difference between success and failure or hope and desperation. When spoken in meanness, they are hard to forget and may cause serious side effects, but when spoken in kindness, words can open the door to a closed heart. They can soften even the unkindest soul. Words are so important.

Kind words live in a special room in the heart. They soothe like a pleasant relaxant, causing enhanced self-esteem, sweet smiles, and secret confidence. They can be magically recalled like a little lifeboat when you're trying to find a way to escape the deep waters of life. If the timing is right, they can serve as wake-up calls to encourage and motivate. Let's all watch what we say and how we say it and remember to be generous with our kind words.

Whether negative or positive, words are the secret to creation. They're like little seeds that bloom into flowers. One good word, just as one bad word, leads to another. Why not check out what you're "planting" by the words you choose to say and see what kind of garden you can grow by using your vocabulary to show someone love today?

The Heart Is No Place
for Resentment

Hurt feelings can make you miserable for days and cause you to carry resentment for a lifetime, if you let them. It's not healthy to bury your emotions or run from them and not process them. It's also not helpful or kind to hurt someone else just because that person hurt you. So you don't say or do something you will regret, try to come up with a plan to deal with your hurt in a beneficial way. When you look back, you want to be pleased rather than embarrassed with the way you handled yourself.

A loving heart has no room for resentment, so holding on to bad feelings is not constructive. People can't unmake their mistakes. If they have asked for forgiveness and tried to make amends, they are more than likely trying to apply their hard lessons to their other experiences in life. Everyone has regrets and we all need second chances. Think about it if you carry bitterness.

We all process everything at our own levels of awareness. If we are too controlled by our emotions and egos, we are more prone to getting our feelings hurt. We need to try to avoid taking things personally so we can become more objective when making judgments. We need to allow other people to live their lives.

One way to deal with resentment is to write out exactly how you feel. No one is going to read what you write but you, so be blatantly honest. Writing about it will take away some of the hurt and help you to get your spirit, mind, and emotions in proper balance. Don't be embarrassed, and always be honest with yourself; your honesty is what will help you to change and mature.

Sometimes your feelings will scream and holler to be shared with the person who hurt you. But it's probably not a good idea to share your hurt then because it's harder to be objective when you're hurting. Take some time to get enough perspective so you can talk about it calmly.

The one thing I know I'll do when my feelings are hurt is not blame the person who hurt me, because I would not be hurt if I hadn't allowed it. That person may not feel he's done anything wrong, for he was just being himself, but I need to do this for myself so I can move on. It is my responsibilty not to own the hurt.

Someone once told me that she'd carried a grudge against me since we were kids over something I'd said that I didn't remember saying. It was silly, but, imagine, that memory had held her hostage for years. I said, "Please forgive me, and let's both learn a lesson… First, let's remember the power of words and let's watch what we say. Second, let's remember who is hurt when we hold a grudge. It's the person carrying it, not the one it's held against." I'm reminded of this lesson every time I'm tempted to hold resentment.

Refuse to be dictated to by your feelings and ego. Put your spirit in authority. Forgive. Don't hold on to resentment. It's just not good for you.

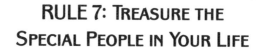

RULE 7: TREASURE THE SPECIAL PEOPLE IN YOUR LIFE

The soul hungers for people to associate with, compare stories with, go places with, and call on the phone. We need people in our lives who are loyal to us and who won't abandon us. We need our families and friends.

Friends are so important because they help balance us, keep us centered, and make us not feel so alone. Family members encourage us, inspire us, and give us confidence. Friends and family teach us about love and help us to have faith.

The special people in our lives create a feeling of unconditional acceptance that allows us to be ourselves. Their acceptance provides security and support and helps us become better people. To have them in our lives to love, learn from, and share life with is a treasure that we never want to lose.

Although we're not able to choose our families the way we do our friends, they can seem like one and the same. A family member can be our friend, and our friend can seem like family. All are appreciated in their own way!

Be There
for Your Family

There's probably no such thing as a perfect family, but our families are with us for the long run. We will be forever connected to them. They have contributed to who we are. They don't just walk in and out of our lives. They're permanent occupants in the rooms of our hearts. We should value our families and not take them for granted.

Ideally, members of our families are always there when we need them. They're in our thoughts, and we're in theirs. They make our lives easier by going the extra mile with us, and they help us understand ourselves better. Be good to them. Some people don't have a family, so those of us who do should realize how lucky we are.

In most cases, our families accept us and make us feel that we belong. They are the ones we call when we're lonesome and need someone to talk to. They understand when we're not perfect, and they usually don't require an explanation. They're quick to forgive, and they encourage us with hopeful words and a helping hand. They get lonesome, too. Stay in close touch.

When others don't know how to care for us, families usually do. They don't pull out when the road of life is not smooth, but they also know when we need the space to be ourselves. They've heard our opinions and they're familiar with our attitudes. They know our strengths and our perceived faults, and they believe with us that our dreams can come true. Always show them that you care.

Value These Gifts of Friendship

Unconditional love... Friends share an unwritten commitment to be there no matter what and to invest however much time and effort are required to be a good friend. Unconditional love is the greatest gift of friendship.

Acceptance... Friends may not agree on everything, but they can talk about almost anything; they embrace each other's differences with fascination rather than with judgment or rejection. They let you be the way you are, without judging you.

Appreciation... Friends never ask more of you than you would give willingly; they don't manipulate you or take you for granted. They show their appreciation convincingly and do things for you that you appreciate.

Support... Friends don't walk the other way when you're hurting. They hang in there with you and pray for you until things are better. They feel like family in your heart.

Someone to confide in... Friends are easy to be with and communicate with. They sense when you need a helping hand and aren't bashful about offering theirs. They don't wait for you to ask.

Someone you can count on... Friends listen, show their concern, and can be depended on and trusted to treat you fairly. There is never a question that they are on your side.

Encouragement... Friends support each other in their dreams; their actions line up with their words that instill confidence. They help you to have courage when you're doubtful.

Loyalty... Friends believe in you and trust you. They have chosen to be committed to each other always, sensitivities and all. They have made a pledge in their hearts to care.

A positive presence... Friends don't say bad things about each other. They show their friendship by the things they say and don't say to you. They are always out to help and not hurt you.

An anchor to keep you steady... Good friends row together against the tide when the world is not making sense, and they help each other not to go crazy along with it. No matter how turbulent the waves, good friends will never give up the "ship." Friendship is the statement that we're not in this world alone.

Choose to Excel
as a Parent

Parenting is a lifetime undertaking. As a guide, guardian, hero, best friend, and your child's main teacher in the school of life, you are called upon to be the best example you can be. Your child will be your greatest blessing and your biggest responsibility. You have created life! Instill in his or her heart early on a deep, abiding respect for the sanctity of life and the value of happiness.

Love your child unconditionally. Express your love by listening, understanding, and showing appreciation. Be patient as he gains experience making decisions, and be loving when she doesn't use the same judgment you think you would.

When in doubt about what to do for your child, ask yourself how you would want your parents to treat you, and be this kind of parent. Encourage dialogue and accountability with your children. When you're about to lose your temper, take a time-out. Be aware of your influence. Someone's listening and watching, and a foundation is being laid. Children learn more by actions than words, more by examples than intention and stories.

Provide your child with a good education. Inspire a love for reading and learning; emphasize the need for goals and priorities and the importance of self-discipline. Teach your child about the value of the work experience, the importance of managing money and starting a savings account, and the significance of building good safety habits. Encourage open dialogue about any subject your child may have questions about, such as sex, drugs, or whatever.

Teach your child the difference between leading and following, between "sowing wild oats" and doing something dangerous. Teach sensitivity and sensibility, caution and common sense. Especially now with the Internet, children are easy prey. Always attend the "Back-to-School" get-togethers for parents. Show your child's teachers that you are there for your child and that you want to assist the teacher in any way you can.

Encourage your child early in life to honor his body, mind, and spirit by making wise food choices, adopting a positive lifestyle, and building healthy, responsible habits. Help your children to see the relationship between cause and effect. Don't lecture; just lead them. Give them more than information. Don't try to make your child into the person you wish you had become but didn't. Assist your children in becoming who they want to be. Teach by example the Golden Rule and the law of love: treat others as you want to be treated and love others as yourself. Show your children the importance of obeying our nation's laws and the consequences of breaking them. Give them whatever information they need so they'll have good references to remember.

As a parent, you have an awesome responsibility. Celebrate this blessing you've been given. Respect your children and be worthy of their respect. Never do anything to make your child doubt your love. Live your life in such a way that someday you can look back and say… "I believe I was the best parent I could have been."

RULE 8: LIFE WILL HURT SOMETIMES, BUT YOU CAN HANDLE IT

Life has its seasons. There will be joy, pain, droughts, heartaches, and rainstorms, but there will also be sunshine, rainbows, happy moments, and smiles. Life will hurt sometimes, but that hurt will eventually become another memory and a lesson learned. Seasons change. Don't let one bad experience influence you unduly.

Look at difficult times as challenges rather than obstacles and as ways to develop patience and maturity. Have confidence in yourself. Don't let your troubles cause you to give up. Befriend them. Learn from them. Come up with constructive ways to handle them. Feel them lose their power over you.

Disappointments sometimes can be blessings in disguise or necessary detours for answers to prayers. Looking at your tears as a potential for growth lessens their pain and sadness over you. And sometimes we just have to trust in life. Who knows? There may be something wonderful headed your way.

Embrace What's Right
Instead of What's Wrong

Believe that... Doors that are closed can also open. Where there's a will, there's also a way. You have the answers inside you to every question you have. Determination gets results, persistence counts, and your attitude matters. You can make a difference in your life and in the world.

Be assured that... There's power in faith, and all things are possible. Thinking and hoping are more important when they give birth to action. You are rewarded for your efforts and your faith. God is on your side, not against you. Your life is a gift to you, but you must take responsibility for its quality.

Trust that... For every negative, there's also a positive. Failure can be the impetus for turning a weakness into a strength. Bad habits can be broken, and progress can be made. You are making a choice, even by doing nothing. When your words and actions are in sync, there's no stopping you.

Realize that... You have power over your thoughts and feelings. You don't have to let your circumstances dictate how you feel. You are equipped to handle whatever you have to. Success is just failure turned around. Change your focus and change your world.

Remember that... You will get back what you give. You will become what you believe. Embrace all that is good. View life as beautiful, and your vision will become like a mirror. Others will see their reflection in you, and you will have come a long way to living well.

When There's No Sunshine in Your Life, Make Your Own

Maybe one of the lessons we can learn from nature is this... it rains on everyone alike... the unlucky and the lucky, the rich and the poor, the joyful and forlorn. Even though we may not choose the circumstances, we do choose how we deal with the "bad weather" in life, and there's always a way we can make the best of it.

If we could look at circumstances a little less personally and a little more objectively, perhaps the storms in our lives wouldn't seem so bad. Maybe the challenges and hardships mean no harm to us but rather are meant to empower us and nourish the soil of our hearts.

We gain power when we choose how we react to things that happen to us. If we choose not to be so afraid, we can learn something from every reality we face. We should not entertain discouragement beyond facing the truth of it and the way to deal with it. With just a slight adjustment, we may be able to turn a negative into something positive. When the dark clouds won't clear, maybe we just need to go inside.

The one thing that is constant is change. When the night never seems to end, tomorrow will come. Time heals. Life goes on. That's just the way it is. Make your best effort and relax. Trust. Refuse to be hopeless.

When you're not happy with the circumstances in your life or with yourself, don't stay out in the rain getting soaked. When there's no sunshine in your life, make your own.

Keep a Steady,
Grounded Perspective

Whether you're at the top or the bottom of your world, remember how you got there. Be sure to thank everyone who helped you on your climb to the top, and get busy moving up if you're at the bottom.

Be thankful for every lesson you learned and every stroke of luck, fate, and circumstance that influenced you on your journey. Carry this attitude of gratitude in your heart. It will serve you well. Find something every day to celebrate. You may not have everything you want, but you can still find things to be thankful for.

If you've done the best you can, be satisfied with your efforts. If you have health problems, focus on your blessings and come up with a plan to do something to help yourself. Your body will respond if you show it that you care. If someone disappoints you, don't let it cause you to lose faith in all people. Just be a little more cautious of whom you allow yourself to trust.

If someone hurts your feelings, don't let it cause you to become hardened. You'd only be hurting yourself. Love anyway. If someone is projecting his or her bias, you don't have to agree with it. It doesn't belong to you.

If you're flying high in the clouds of triumph or buried alive in the agony of defeat, keep a steady, grounded perspective. No matter what you're going through, be prepared for the worst, expect the best, and realize it's all a part of life. Know that you can handle whatever comes your way.

Pep Talk on Avoiding Discouragement

Look at your life as a journey and enjoy the ride. Get the most out of the detours, and when things happen that you didn't plan, regroup.

Do your best, but if what you've been doing isn't working, try a different approach. Be passionate about the process, but don't be too attached to the outcome. A certain amount of life is out of our hands.

Wish the best for everyone. Applaud someone else's win as much as you would your own. Be an encourager, and encouragement will find its way back to you.

Trust that there's a divine plan. We may not always know what's best for us. A disappointment now could mean a victory later, so don't be discouraged when life hands you a surprise or refuses to cooperate with your wishes. It may have its own timetable that would also be in your own best interest, and there may be a good reason for the delay in reaching your goals.

Ask no more of yourself than the best that you can do, and be satisfied with that. Be compassionate toward yourself as well as others.

Don't relive something after it's done; it's out of your hands, too late, over! Learn the lesson and move on. Refuse to be discouraged for long. The longer you stay down, the harder it will be to get up. Get over it.

Have the attitude that no one, except you, owes you anything. Give without expecting a thank-you in return. But when someone does something for you, be appreciative of even the smallest gesture.

Choose your thoughts and your feelings or they will choose you; they can free you or keep you bound. Educate your spirit and give it authority over your mind and your emotions. Listen to your heart, and have faith that all things will work together for your good. Doing the right thing doesn't always feel good, but it will feel right. If your mind and spirit are in disagreement, listen to your spirit. It knows things your mind may not know.

After you've done all you can, sometimes you just need to trust life. Once, George "Goober" Lindsey, probably best known for his role on *The Andy Griffith Show*, asked me to write him a song, so I did; but I also pitched him "Funny Face." He recorded the song I wrote for him, but because he didn't record "Funny Face," I almost became discouraged. A short time after, I thanked God and George that he didn't because it sold over a million copies and became my second number-one single. What we are sorry about today sometimes we'll be glad about tomorrow. Life knew better than I what was best for me.

So life is a process, a journey. Always keep hope alive. Realize that things will be different tomorrow, but believe that things will also be better and you can make a difference.

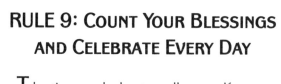

RULE 9: COUNT YOUR BLESSINGS AND CELEBRATE EVERY DAY

Take time each day to pull yourself away from all the noise and look around you. Appreciate those who have enhanced the quality of your life. Remember that you're in their lives for a reason, too; you're just as valuable to them. Life's a two-way street. Don't take your blessings for granted.

You can't give more than you have or be someone you're not; you can only be you. Accept yourself and do your best. Keep up the good work. Commit to doing whatever you're led to do. Know when to start and when to stop, when to lead and when to follow.

Look at each day as twenty-four hours to treasure and make the best of. Yesterday is gone and can't be changed, the present is what you have right now, and the future is bright and full of promise and opportunities. Learn to live your life one day at a time, to find the good in everything, and to appreciate every minute of every day.

Think About All the Ways
You Are Blessed

You are blessed if you feel a close and constant connection to your Creator, if you can enjoy nature and this remarkable universe, and if you are in touch with the inspiration and love in your heart so you can discover your own power.

You are blessed if you can feel no prejudice toward others, treat others in a way that encourages and lifts them up, and show love in a way that can be received by others.

You are blessed if you can hold your tongue in a fit of anger, wait until you have some balance on the issue at hand to process it, and if you can come to terms with it in such a way that you can learn from it.

You are blessed if you can admit truths to yourself instead of running from them, covering them up, or playing games so you don't have to face them. You are blessed if you can see how truth is a cleanser for your soul and an important vehicle for change, not something to be ashamed or afraid of.

You are blessed if you can forgive others quickly and not let bad feelings fester and make you feel miserable. You are blessed if you can forgive yourself each time some disappointment or conflict comes back into your mind.

You are blessed if you can give without expecting others to live up to your expectations, for each time you give with an unselfish attitude is a measure of your own integrity.

Don't Worry So Much...

Everyone has fears, troubles, and unmet needs, but worrying about them will usually only delay your progress, not further it. Worrying takes away concentration that you could put to better use. It recycles the same old fears, and you wind up spinning in place like you've done a hundred times before.

If you've taken whatever action you can to address your concerns, it's time to rest and get your mind on something else. Find an activity that you enjoy and that you can be totally engaged in. If you find that you still worry, at least restrict the amount of time that you do. Schedule "worry time." For instance, you could say that your worry times are 10:00 and 5:00 for five minutes each. You can worry as much as you can for those five-minute segments, but no more.

Surrender Your Stubbornness...

You may experience stubbornness when faced with criticism, disagreement, or rejection. If you put your heart and soul into something, you want others to feel the same way you do and to see things through your eyes, but they can't. They only have their feelings and their eyes. You may find yourself resisting any suggestion to change course, and though you may need to, you might not want to cooperate. No one likes to be corrected, especially against his or her will, but sometimes we have to address our attitudes and not let stubbornness win. Otherwise, the result we get might not be worth anything.

A heart that harbors stubbornness leaves little room for creativity and inspiration. It's okay to "stew" about something for a while, but as soon as possible, surrender your stubbornness and humble yourself to start over with a willing mind and a fresh perspective. Your heart will soon open to light and joy.

Be Slow to Anger...

When anger rules the mind, hate takes over the heart. It's a dead-end street that can damage people, joy, hope, peace, relationships, and the opportunity to heal.

Find a healthy way to process anger so it doesn't destroy the love in your heart and take control of your senses. Even though someone else may have provoked it, the anger is inside you, and you must deal with it as yours, not as a reason to blame someone else.

Find a practical way to argue. Agree to disagree without judgment. If you need to scream and holler, do it so no one else can hear you. Count to ten. Just get it out of you as fast as you can without hurting someone else or yourself. Remember that anger is the flip side of joy, and you can turn this energy around.

Let Go of Guilt...

When you say or do something you wish you could take back... when you don't live up to your expectations of yourself... when you don't keep commitments... when you're not as good as your word... when you don't reciprocate with equal consideration or you don't treat someone fairly... when you're not as generous as you know you could be... these are only some of the scenarios that can set the stage to hold on to guilt.

We hang on to guilt to punish ourselves for our own perceived wrongdoings, but if it doesn't lead to something productive, it's a waste of your power and energy. Alter your behavior to avoid falling into the same trap again. Honor your relationships by keeping your word and sharing openly and honestly with people. Apologize and admit your mistake quickly; your apology will help you and the person you may have hurt feel better. Then forgive yourself. Let go of your guilt.

Live Your Life
One Day at a Time

A child grows into adulthood one day at a time. A tree grows one branch at a time. A destination is reached one mile at a time. A job is completed one task at a time. A song is written one word and one note at a time. A dream comes true one step at a time.

Instead of being critical of yourself for all the things you haven't gotten done in years, focus on doing the best you can today. Sometimes we waste more time dreading to start something than it would actually take to do the job.

Make a "to-do" list of what you want to accomplish and consider the amount of time you have for each project you undertake. Set your priorities. Don't take on more than you can handle. Do one small task at a time. Give yourself credit when you make progress.

You're reinforcing a negative opinion of yourself by entertaining nagging thoughts about what you haven't done. I say to myself sometimes, "Either do it or shut up about it." Sneak up on yourself one day and start somewhere… doing one job at a time. It probably won't take you as long as you think.

You'll be more relaxed, less stressed, and happier if you strive to make the best out of every single hour and if you learn to live your life one day at a time. Once you adopt this attitude, you'll breathe a real sigh of relief.

Make Every Day
a Great Day to Be Alive

Look at each day as your very own garden. Sow the right seeds to achieve your goals. Nurture your seeds appropriately, and believe that they'll grow and bloom into the most beautiful flowers you've ever seen. Don't dig them up with doubts. Growth occurs in the root before it can be seen with the eye. In other words, nourish your hopes with faith, or you may stunt their growth.

Don't waste time being anxious. Just let your heart and mind lead you to act on your own best advice to yourself. Release the rest. Be satisfied with doing your part. Allow yourself to daydream and fantasize. Look forward to every day with great anticipation. Don't be afraid to break your routine and explore a little. If you feel stuck, make some new wishes and dream some new dreams. Rediscover yourself. Review all the happy times that have made you who you are. Reflect on the lessons you've learned from the mistakes you've made. Accept them rather than look on them with regret.

Find something to enjoy in everything you do. If you give joyfully, you are making a deposit in your blessings account, the account that gives back to you what you've sown. If you're not excited about your life, you're cheating yourself. You might not be able to do everything, but you can do something. Start every day by being glad that you're alive. The rest will take care of itself.

RULE 10: CHOOSE TO BE HAPPY

We just get one trip through this life, and with all the detours and surprises and bumps in the road, it's hard not to be unhappy and miserable some of the time. If you can't change the circumstances, change the way you look at them. Just a shift in your attitude can change frustration to fascination.

Happiness is the joy in your soul finding its smile. It's opening your heart and allowing love to live there and affect everything you do. Happiness is being good to others and trying to make a worthwhile difference. It's realizing that none of us is perfect. It's a feeling that you know who you are, why you're here, and that, no matter what happens, you're going to be all right.

Even if you seem to have more obstacles than windows of opportunity, you can choose to be joyful. Decide that life is good and you are special. Decide not to put off enjoying life because everything's not perfect. Steadfastly refuse to let anything steal your joy. Choose to be happy... and you will be!

Be Inspired by New Hopes and Possibilities

See the beauty in nature and recognize your own worth. You may not have everything you want, but you've got you!

This world is a crazy place, but you can find the ways that life is great. Lose the tight schedule, breathe easy, and rest a little. Think about your past and your future; look at how far you've come and where you want to go. When you feel yourself getting stressed and worried, stop and say, "Relax. I can't do this any faster."

If you find yourself feeling down, don't forget that there's a field of positive energy surrounding you, just waiting for you to engage it, but you have to go there. Play in this field. Believe the best of yourself and others. Give yourself every chance you deserve. Think possible, not impossible. The best is yet to come. Believe it!

Always remember: Life is for dancing... in the street, on a cloud, in some room in your mind. It's for remembering the happy moments and the answered prayers. It's for singing... your favorite song, the song in your heart, the whatever-makes-you-feel-good song. It's for receiving lots of love, good wishes, and special words of praise. Life is for dreaming dreams and making them come true. Life is for living... and giving... and believing... in God, in love, in people, and in yourself.

Count your blessings, and share your life with your favorite people. Love others, and remind yourself that you are appreciated and loved, too... because you are.

Believe

There are rainbows and pots of gold ahead for you... opportunities to explore, puzzles to solve, and hopes and dreams to ponder.

Catch these pieces of life as they come, and hold them close to you. Savor every triumph, and learn from every failure. Be courageous. Be passionate. Enjoy the ride, chase every quest, and praise every hint of answers to your questions. Dream big. Work hard. Enjoy your play time. Deal with all the struggles in life with the attitude of a winner and the heart of a champion. You may not always get what you want, but you're never a failure if you give it your all and do the best you can.

Don't let one task or one result define you. Don't let one mistake make you think you've lost the war when it was only a single battle. Let your mistakes teach you. Everyone makes them. Be receptive enough to recognize an opportunity you might not have imagined, and be flexible enough to change your direction if you need to. Welcome the challenges. Stay strong and committed to your goals. Believe that you are up to the task.

Let your imagination take you to that perfect place where there is nothing to be afraid of and you can have anything you want. Prepare yourself. Knock on the door of opportunity and be ready when it answers. Celebrate all the possibilities. Your destiny calls. Embrace it. Be good. Believe in miracles. Accept that all things are possible. Love and allow yourself to be loved. Reach for the stars, go for your dreams, and make your life as happy as it can be.

Your Future Is Now...
Go for It!

Life is meant to be savored and enjoyed; it's not a video game to be played casually or decided by the push of a button. The world is changing quickly, but the things that really matter are the things that don't change. Seek what is lasting — love, knowledge, and justice.

Love will always be the biggest deal of all. Love others just as they are. Don't judge them or try to change them. Their lives are their own, just as your life is your own. Love yourself just as you are. Change what you need to and accept the rest. There's no one like you. You have a purpose here.

The secret to making right decisions is knowledge. Inform yourself and act according to what you believe is right. Don't imitate someone else just because others do.

Search your heart and listen to what it's saying to you. It will always be your most trustworthy source of light. Express your own unique beauty and become the person you want to be. Respect your own thoughts, even when they are not in agreement with others. Don't sell yourself to the highest bidder. Know what you want out of life and go after it.

Seek justice for all mankind. Stand up for what you believe. Treat others fairly, not as they treat you. Enjoy your cell phones and computers, but don't ignore the face-to-face exchanges. Be grateful for kindnesses paid to you, and don't forget to say thank you.

Your future starts now. Have fun. Study hard. Be good. Love everyone, including yourself.

We Need Each Other

We are all part of the world family, and as a society, we need to feel our significance to our planet and to each other. We should have the right to live our lives as we choose so long as we harm no one.

Most of us are doing the best we can with our given situations. Each time we see someone who is succeeding at something we're trying to do, their success encourages us. When we meet people who are courteous and willing to offer a helping hand, they make us feel connected. When someone has time to listen to what we have to say and to treat us with respect and kindness, we are inspired to try to better ourselves and make a difference in our community. We need to reach out to each other and give what we can when we can. We need understanding and compassion when something goes wrong. We need to be good to each other.

No matter how different we may be, we need to respect each other. Differences are natural, and we can learn a lot by accepting each other's differences. We're not robots. Diversity is healthy; it is one of the joys of our freedom. We all need a family that we can belong to and a place where we are free to be ourselves. We need to feel that there is hope, safety, and justice, and we need to have pride in this place we call home.

I encourage you to think about what you really believe and allow your beliefs to empower you to do good in this society that needs so much light and love and vision now. I believe we all know what is right and what is wrong. I have a lot of confidence in us, and I hope we don't let ourselves down. We need each other!

May You Have Many Bright Tomorrows

May you be blessed with good health and happiness. May your guardian angels protect you, keep you safe from harm, and blanket you with joy, contentment, peace, and prosperity.

May you be guided with the wisdom to make choices that will enhance your life and the awareness to make changes that are in your best interest. Remember, the secret to achieving anything is in your heart, and your decisions should be *your* choices. Change emanates from the inside out when you allow love to help you. Like us, love doesn't want to impose or be where it's not wanted, so it will wait silently in the wings until you recognize it and let it help you achieve your full potential.

May you reach that magical combination of confidence and humility, effort and relaxation, reality and optimism... all the things that will give you wings for your flight as you pursue your purpose. May you have a storehouse of opportunities, the ability to meet your goals, and the satisfaction of your own approval and acceptance. May you have a strong spirit and a willing mind. May your heart be filled with love to help you become all you want to be and overcome anything that holds you back.

Always remember that you're someone very special. Show the world your loving heart, and don't be afraid to encourage others, for what you give, you'll get back. You have a purpose here. Wrap your arms around life and challenge yourself to be boldly and beautifully you. May there be wonders waiting around every corner and rainbows across your sky as you go now and make a positive difference in this crazy, mixed-up world.

About the Author

With her first album, *The Happiest Girl in the Whole U.S.A.*, which achieved platinum album status and earned her a Grammy, Donna Fargo established herself as an award-winning singer, songwriter, and performer. Her credits include seven Academy of Country Music Association awards, five Billboard awards, fifteen Broadcast Music Incorporated (BMI) writing awards, and two National Association of Recording Merchandisers awards for bestselling artist. She has also been honored by the Country Music Association, the National Academy of Recording Arts and Sciences, and the Music Operators of America, and she was the first inductee into the North America Country Music Association's International Hall of Fame. As a writer, her most coveted awards, in addition to the Robert J. Burton Award that she won for "Most Performed Song of the Year," are her Million-Airs Awards, presented to writers of songs that achieve the blockbuster status of 1,000,000 or more performances.

Prior to achieving superstardom and becoming one of the most prolific songwriters in Nashville, Donna was a high school English teacher. It is her love of the English language and her desire to communicate sincere and honest emotions that compelled Donna to try her hand at writing something other than song lyrics. Donna's other books include *Trust in Yourself, I Prayed for You Today,* and *To the Love of My Life.* Her writings also appear on Blue Mountain Arts greeting cards, calendars, and other gift items.